EVERYDAY WRITING:
A Deconstruction of the Human Hive

By Nathaniel Watts

© 2013 Watts Is What

4

Everyday Writing: A Deconstruction of the Human Hive

ISBN 978-061592809-8

Library of Congress Control Number:

2013922784

Published by

Watts Is What
P.O. Box 1382, N. Massapequa, NY 11758

EVERYDAY WRITING:
A Deconstruction of the Human Hive

CREDITS

Cover Design:

Nick Romano, Nate watts

Main Text Edits:

Nate Watts, Corey Larkin

Introduction Edits:

Nate Watts, Sandy Lynn Riefberg

Pretext and Postscript Edits:

Nate Watts

Text Layout:

Nate Watts, Nick Romano, Scott Greer

Nathaniel Watts is available for either solo or band performances. For booking information contact: **booking@wattsiswhat.com**

Facebook: **facebook.com/everydaywriting. Also, find the book and give it a:**

YouTube: **youtube.com/wattsiswhat**

Thank you to everyone who helped bring this vision to life, especially Nick and Scott. Your commitments will never be forgotten.

photo credit: Chester Cacace

Maybe it's the color of the sun cut flat
An' cov'rin' the crossroads I'm standing at
Or maybe it's the weather or something like that
But Mama, you just on my mind

-B. Dylan

photo credit: Nate Watts

Friday September 27, 2013 7:12am Monroe, NY:

Currently I'm on the main lawn of Ananda Ashram staring over a thriving unfished lake. The founder of this magical place is Shri Brahmananda Sarasvati. He left physical form around 20 years ago. His soul will shine here for eternity. Perhaps that's why he's listed as the place's present spiritual director. Constant transmissions from the other side make his teachings beyond credible.

I've been at the ashram for five days to begin final edits on the project in your hands right now. I was told I'd find reality here. I didn't look, but it sure found me. The poor thing is beaten and frail due to accumulating attempts of sabotage. Dangerous elements are part of its makeup. Mind…body…soul… nature…truth, Consensus strives to distract us from such things.

Everyone is expected to live in paved developments, get up for work and eat shitty pseudo foods. In between there's time for television and technology designed to seduce minds and remove them from a natural environment. In turn, individuals seem to lose individuality. Entrapping people within bullshit domains of frivality allows for advancement of the assimilation process.

A hive begins through establishing a colony of drones and the human hive is no exception. While struggling within its catacombs, it's obvious to see how sameness is blanketing US. It is a plague gnawing on our subconscious minds to impose an expected mode of behavior. Instead of being encouraged to find our I-amness, we are more so told "**YOU** are this."

We are not a hive in the sense of being one species working toward the betterment of a colony. No, our structure is set up for us to always compete. The objective is to have failure dominate. Failures are easy to oppress and keep working for the betterment of powers that most will never see or know of.

Yeah...I have a tendency of going deep. Perhaps, right now, you're wondering who I am and what the fuck this project is. Well, none of that is easy, but the latter is a better starting point.

Everyday Writing: A Deconstruction of the Human Hive is my résumé. It's an application for a job that I may be the only one applying for. The question is: does the public want the position filled?

These pages contain thoughts on observations from a societal outcast covering the beat. It's the beat of you, the beat of me, the beat of US moving further forward into a new era of existence. We're already oldtimers thanks to a 1900-sumtin birth date. The children from this century will remind us of that when their dominance begins seven years from now. The 20-tykes they are. Us relics will be in their way. Unease develops when thinking about what fully hived humans will be like, yet I aspire to one day become a college professor.

Why am I talking so much about the future? Now is where minds to be! These times are ours and I don't understand why so few care to document them. Our feelings, thoughts, concerns, cares, likes, loves and dislikes are not being conveyed. I feel them, though, in between globs of hate and confusion

Nearly every day I clear my mind of thought, enter a trance state and attempt to inhale the essence of what's in the air. Then it's exhaled through word. Often my fingers cruise across a keyboard to punch out words striking my brain that second. What's recorded is not retained. It's often discovered months after when I need new material for readings and band performances

Everything began on March 6, 2011. The exact time is unfortunately lost in mountains of used minutes. It marked the moment I became determined to make something of myself through writing. For that to happen, it needs to be done as every day as possible. I logged the date by typing the month to discover how MS Word automatically fills out the rest...cool. It became a motivational factor to make sure few days get missed. Once 11:59pm closes that program goes right to a date change.

I saved the first entry as "everyday writing." At the time, it was viewed as a forum for me to write daily scratch and discover an eventual project. As the progression continued, it became evident that this is the project. What triggered that realization is the opening piece of the pretext.

No, don't think we start from 2011. Our journey begins where beliefs had the world ending- December 21, 2012. The pretext is present to show aspects of *Everyday Writing*'s past. Broader strokes were applied then. That first piece in many ways is like the single for a concept album.

To fully describe *Everyday Writing* is to say what it isn't. This is not a journal! Yes, it is laid out in journal form but there is no daily personal crap. Sometimes events of a day are recorded, but, often, what's written maintains its own relevance. Of course, with the dates being incorporated, you can explore for potential inspirations.

This is most definitely not a collection of poetry! Yes, poetics are often used. I'd go as far as saying that a small handful of these 104 thoughts are legitimate poems but any laureate of that craft would disassociate this project from their genre. At the same time, I'm often called a poet.

Personally, I wish it was fiction. Some may say it is. I hope you do. I don't want people agreeing with most of what's in here. I want ya's to question. Come to your own conclusions and tell me I'm wrong!! But if you do, don't simply say so. Whatever you think, please don't call me a poet.

In regards to the final product, people tell me that a brain splitting effect develops when attempting to read it straight through. Take your time. This is a work that you can put down and come back to. And, yeah, the joke has been circulating as to what room it's suitable for.

Entries are marked by their date and times. The start time is at the top and the end is marked in an old journalism method. While attending J-school, I was shown how submitted pieces would close with #30#. This way through the editing and layout process everyone knew where a story finished. I replaced that 30 with the completion time and date (if different from the start time's) and opted to incorporate it. You'll also notice that the right side of the text is all jagged. I left it like that to have the same look as when it's on my monitor. Then text fonts change at points. It's easy to realize why.

Also, there is a line above each piece for you to add your own title, notes or whatever. I think the mixture of words and numbers says a lot. Weird and revealing things happen. I'm interested in hearing what astrologers, numerologists and you readers discover. My time at the ashram has made me realize how much of what is written here only pecks into greater infinite knowledge. There is so much to cover and uncover.

Everyday Writing has pushed me since its creation. I never had an idea of where to start it as a release until the most powerful day I've lived to date, which is not where we start. No, if you remember, come sunrise December 21, 2012 we were supposed to get hit with solar flares, pole shift and an array of catastrophes capable of wiping this planet clean. Unrest was bubbling the closer it came.

I was affixed on that end factor. In my writings a 100 day countdown began toward its arrival. I was not focused on the possibilities. I saw a need to encapsulate the hysteria surrounding them. Once the 21st closed, I should have always focused on it as a starting point. Instead, I wrote that in the day's entry only to lose sight. A fresh epoch has begun. The ancients knew this. I know a whole lot has not felt same since. Plenty of chaos has followed. Recording the first six months of this young unnamed age shows an adventure I was unaware of until a few weeks ago.

There are characters in this book! I had no idea of that until backtracking. They're reoccurring entities such as demons, consensus and our over-seers. Those types are playing too much of a role in where we are right now- us watching the deterioration of the final vertebrae supporting US. Big, horrible things seem to be simmering toward a global boil. We were hoodwinked to allow them. Now I feel it's important to document the feelings and views left in their wake. What will define our times is everything everyone is trying to look away from.

This premier installment is self-published. I've gotten a lot of flack for that. People are already not taking me serious. I want to make clear that I have never once solicited this project to any publisher. The reasons for that are, first off, I was really in no mood to wait two years for rejection letters. This is something that has to be released now. Second, I doubted any worthwhile publishing company would take a chance on it. *Everyday Writing* and its author are two scary things to invest in- different and new. Finally, if accepted, it would come with the risk of restraint.

Everyday Writing needs to prove itself. It's you readers who will determine its fate and if a second installment comes to be. I'm broke, there is no promo budget. Your Web reviews will be the only coverage it receives. Your words are what will keep these words alive.

Our adventure here ends on the first day of summer '13. If given the opportunity to write a second installment, I know we will not be picking up from the next day because I missed it (damn!). I have an insane amount of material from the past and present that I can always whip into something, but I already envision the next one.

I plan on traveling anywhere I can to sign up for open mics and introduce myself to new cities and citizens. In doing so, I'll be living within the hive more than ever. Those experiences will enable this project to grow and become more relevant.

So, I suppose in order for me to get this gig, I should reveal a bit more about the main character. His story, though, would take up too much space for an intro. If a need arises to express more, I have plans to submit to forums like the Moth reading series (moth.org) and maybe even one crazy book. But let's start here: people think they have something on him, but they only know what was once known. One's past and present seldom align with perfection, but his has a disconnect. Shit happens that leads to change. People will say he survived a suicidal breakdown. I'll tell ya he didn't make it. Oh, are you wondering what that makes him? Well…..... Watts is what.

When living in dark times, there is a need to hold on to light.

Om shanti

#8:30am#

photo credit: Nate Watts

Pretext- *EVERYDAY WRITING: A Deconstruction of the Human Hive*

Sunday April 10, 2011 10:11pm:

Chaos rains down as piss from demons. Their tinkles carry a virus. When one gets the bug a cure is hard to achieve. We know there's a need to cleanse and are aware of how, but the act of freeing ourselves is hardly a quick blink and deep breath. No! It involves efforts that seem too challenging. In choosing not to pursue them, you become another victim. Then you get used until your scrappy remains renew the dirt of this Earth; a planet paved into a world beyond what it was supposed to be. That there is what allows disorder to flourish. Minds are not a construction for confinement. Eyes are not a design to view screens and our hands did not develop to type as much as masturbate. All of us are prone to madness from living within a synthetic infrastructure that's getting more frigid as the digital grows more diligent. Forget about cold blooded. There is no heart! There's only a quasi brain devoid of any sense but to carry out commands that, at times, its programmers can not morally perform. Yeah, this chaos is growing into a relentless tempest. Those prone to it are considered ill, insane or inefficient, but how can anyone adapt to a domain so far from our point of origin?

#10:35pm#

Friday May 13, 2011 11:34pm:_____

Superstition is for the stupid and clothing defines the confined! Supposedly Neanderthals were the first to have this textile epiphany. Well, kudos to the cave man! Though I have no doubt that when back in his dwelling, that bearskin gave way to BARE skin as he went on to bareback his bucktoothed, big boobed babe before his brethren and the rest not giving a damn. Attire led to us homos overcoming various meteorological conditions and in turn became the key tool toward our global domination. Unfortunately, it's now mandatory. The natural form is a form of taboo. Nudity gives proof that we are the most awkward looking creature. It reminds the subconscious of origins it's ashamed of and leads to it stroking the conscious with silly messages stressing... divinity. Reality displays a convoluted DNA network that could've easily been the result of inbreeding crossbreeds at a higher level than our own kind has with the creation of such ridiculous organisms as the bubble-eyed goldfish. This DNA goo is a tool within itself. Like any implement, a weapon element is well intact. High powered pods sit in scrotums cocked and ready for turbo ejaculations. Every squirt is designed to continue mass infestation.

#11:56pm#

Tuesday May 1, 2012 11:59pm:

The warmth of yet another summer begins its seasonal domination, but heat of another sort is rising faster. Winter wasn't enough to exterminate and now it's set to burst into the fields. These pastures, though, are ones of societal structure. Revolutionary energy is what I am referring to and the people creating it have a goal of disruption. It's needed to gain attention and support in their battle of taking down the nemesis. Their chances of success are nearly nil. It's as if all is being done to reveal a collapse of the fundamental foundation our nation sprouted from. The grand architects of yesteryear would erupt with rage in seeing what their creation has grown into. Laws are flying from the Hill to points where few are innocent in the land of the free. Amongst the crumbling infrastructure pristine, overly efficient detention centers already rise. Is what has been foreseen coming to be? A constitutional collapse is on the horizon giving way to a totalitarian state that will eliminate even dreams had while living the nightmare. Who takes control is insignificant. Such a being is only a puppet. All of them have different moves, but the master never changes. Who is it? WHO?! Dammit, the clutch is becoming more apparent but the hand hides within an invisible glove. Reveal yourself you ancient serpent!! How much strength can you have if there's always a need to remain nameless?

#May 2, 2012 12:13am#

photo credit: Nate Watts

EVERYDAY WRITING:
A Deconstruction of the Human Hive (December 21, 2012 - June 21, 2013)

A psychic once warned me about spirits, but I can warn you about psychics...

Friday December 21, 2012 1:12am:_____

Autumn fades within hours, yet some annuals live in full bloom including an impatient. It may become the last of its kind. The recent arrival of a mold, fungus or something is contaminating the genus. Such is Earth's way. Extinction exists to counteract existence. The process seems to be accelerating. Within hours nothingness may prevail. Do we survive this day or is there a need to document the final hours of our kind? Well, for everything to happen because of one sunrise would be like getting the gastro as opposed to working it off. We've done enough to this world that its demise is likely. More needs to be achieved.

11:55am

So the sun shines with enough ferocity to remind us how it can kill, but we live yet another 24hr period. This one brings forth a new winter. The seasons continue their usual cycle. Our eminent power star still sets west. Yet, within these past 100 days enough has gone down where much won't be the same. Doubleplusungood residents have done us in. The many are soon to experience radical reverberations following actions of a select few. Do any of us know those individuals? Are we to think that crazed disobedient bastards live in every neighborhood? Must we insist on preemptive measures to stop them? Now that our kind is still alive are we to always believe the words of the Vatican, NASA, the Whitehouse? Yeah, they know how to keep US safe, but is that the same as us living?

7:51pm

It's time to begin again. Born within winter's darkness a fresh phase arrives. We have entered a new starting point on an Earth orbiting within depths of a universe we know too little about. Too many deem we're alone within it. Something happened today. As time transpires, it will reveal itself more. We will eventually notice, perhaps not its origins, but certainly the aftermath. Then again, we are expected to live oblivious.

#8:01pm#

Tuesday December 25, 2012 4:50pm:_____

Outside, a silent abandon resonates. Indoors, people are junkies getting stoned on upbeat energy. It's what this day is about. The religion laying claim is an intruder! Higher-ups placed their highest power on pre-existing foundation to demolish old gods; one hollow statue replacing another. This day possesses a distinct energy. That is knowledge known since our dawn. We serve as the transmitters to keep it flowing. Emissions of positivity build through rejoicing. Family energy charges it. Love makes it grow. Melancholy, it seeps through. That's right...on this day good tidings zip as cheery atoms. The aim is to create fatty molecules of happy humanity as an insulative layer in preparation for winter death. Are we really that empathetic? The answer must be yes. Only then can it explain how well we can hurt.

#5:02pm#

Wednesday December 26, 2012 11:21pm:_____

Yeah, it's Boxing Day. The modern version of it rocks! It marks the beginning of retailers putting away crappy décor set up to inspire that synthetic fa-la-la feel. Box that shit up until another August! Ah, August you lovely lazy month. It feels so long before your reign. Then when you come, there's not much to long for. Your flaring temps have been culling out the weak and may one day do in everyone. D'oh! Doomsday talk is over isn't it? Well, we are told that we will not know the hour or day. That same power tells us to live submissively. Is it so others can live freely? We have no idea what (insert upcoming year) has to offer but whatever is in store will give rise to some things that will lead to the fall of others and the innocent will remain victim.

Circles, well… ellipticals, are what these words become. The same topics always find their way back around. Hopefully the wording gets stronger, but such things do not matter. I have no readers as of now. There's a need to remain incognito. If exposed too soon I will be disposed of. I know nothing, except for one thing which is what most attempts are made to distract US from.

#11:38pm#

Thursday December 27, 2012 11:59pm:_____

December's fade brings with it the harvest of good souls. Their time arrives for them to guide a parade of what winter wants. Buoyant energy produces a year's final bits of warmth to stroke our inner selves. As it travels there is hope to preserve the cycles of life from total corruption but the supply is getting scarce. Too much stock rots before expiration. Pills keep more folks alive but few seem happy about it. Negativity seeps through the sadness of still being beings. Life does affect death. However personification ceases when the soul is released. It's surely a freeform affair. The energy inside is the true you. Feel it! Become one with it! Once you do is when you find self.

#Friday December 28, 2012 12:11am#

Sunday December 30, 2012 11:37pm:_____

Spin, spin the black circle and when that baby goes, play it loud! Live within those grooves and let the sound waves take you from the domain that surrounds. Keep in mind, as round and round it goes, forward is the only way this globe knows. Spin, spin we do every day without a clue. Is there a need to wonder why the world is so dizzying? Muddled-up mental frequencies fill the air. They mesh to distort our key source of function- emotion. The brain needs to feel and manufactures feelings by what it has been exposed to and how treated. The person becomes conditioned to believe that this is how it will always be. Songs serve as surrogates to get us through. Demons rule these times. Misery is their oxygen. To maintain healthy production, their most powerful attack is the corruption of love.

2012 is lingering to the point where it has no relevance. People want it forgotten. It's filled with letdowns and lost hopes.

#Monday December 31, 2012 12:00am#

Monday December 31, 2012 7:07pm: _____

Nothing fully means what it is and I doubt there's one person who is truly that. However there is only a full something in some ones and that means anyone who has found self. Electricity glowing in the face shows a person fully in touch. The individual is then ready for the road and forward is the only way they know because it's the only way to go.

Marijuana makes the music.

#7:27pm#

Tuesday January 1, 2013 11:13pm:

Here we stand within a year that many believed would never come. In turn it marks an end to old times. New is a calendar for a renewed world. We want to see it bright and free of yesteryear decay. However, what is desired may not be willed. There must be an unfulfilled addiction to progress in order to experience success.

#11:20pm#

Friday January 4, 2013 11:36pm:

A true magician does not use tricks. If he did, it would be as petty as a comedian with knock-knock jokes. The real ones make their visions manifest. How? HAHAHA...you know that never gets revealed. At times the magic goes unnoticed. It seems natural. Certain acts are derived from the creator for him to bridge gaps to his destiny. As his powers grow they carry him and make people realize what he is. Others will say otherwise. They only know what he was. There lies the magic.

#11:51pm#

Saturday January 5, 2013 10:49pm:_____

Cures too often get refused by those who ail because the human brain is hostage to consensus. It no longer pursues what it needs as much as what is approved. If the food smells or looks funny, well that shit can't be good for ya. Herbs are overlooked in favor of the pills and living within a wrath of confusion always overrides meditation. Our kind exists under a pretension of superiority simply because it goes unchallenged. In other words, we are the best killers! We can snag magnificent, fierce fish to get thrills out of watching their perfect bodies hang out of their element while folks gather round for prize shots. If elephants had opposable thumbs they would be the masters. Singletrunkedly they could conquer anyone anywhere. However, those thoughts would never arise in their advanced brains. All they'd want is what they want- to live undisturbed. Instead we slaughter them. I mention what I say because we are dumb. We have been manipulated to become dimwitted, submissive and conditioned to allow our impressionable inner animal prevail. Superior life does exist! Proof has been present since the times of Sumer. Doubt remains because of what Consensus stresses. Dare an attempt be made to advance from our current neotenic phase. It feels as if we've been sentenced to it. Consensus keeps US from curing. Consensus keeps US from realizing. Consensus keeps US under control through extracting the esoteric from exoteric realms.

#11:20pm#

It's the beat.
It's always about the beat.
It's the beat that never ends
It goes as frequent as our hearts.
They beat independent of one another
but always search for unity.
Our hearts beat longing to open.
Our hearts beat longing to open.
We forget that demons rule these times.
Misery is their oxygen.
To maintain healthy production,
their most powerful attack is
the corruption of love.
Yet our hearts beat longing to open

Sunday January 6, 2013 11:58pm:

The times of groovy will always remain preserved in film, print and any future medium. They're reran, reran and reran before our eyes and make us feel as if the world is still that. Oh, I ramble nonstop about what is out there, but what lies inside you? What does your inner self believe? I'm nearly certain that love is somehow involved. It's a resilient power that transcends any barrier but...it's blind. Why share it? Why release it? Too often it's deemed undesirable by the targeted recipient. Use it to connect with your familiars! They will always give more back. Mold it into bonds of friendship! Those always seem stronger. Never hide it from your mother!! But expecting another person to return a full force blow to develop a prized connection??? That's when your self's value depletes. That's when you make yourself pathetically vulnerable. That's when joy is taken by the other in shredding it. That's when you start feeding demons. We are never issued a right to love and there is surely no mandate for it to be returned. So why expect it? Yes, the love generation has aged and too much has gone sour. Doom more often prevails.

#Monday January 7, 2013 12:26am#

Yet our hearts beat longing to open

Monday January 7, 2013 12:03pm:_____

Spirit energy surrounds me. My soul interconnects with ones who have already found their way. A cluster arrived today to present fragments of my future. What, is for me to know and my mission to fulfill. Finding yours can be a simple meditation away. Yeah, that is considered silly talk. It amuses me. It's funny seeing Consensus administer religions with strong emphasis on afterlife then choose not to acknowledge those who live past living. Then it is absolutely fuckin' hilarious how these high holy powers never mention a need to cleanse **and caress** the soul. That should be done as often as tending to genitalia. Instead, psalms are stressed. Afterlife is some candy coated tale said to be left in determination of respective almighties. Heaven and hell are not places! All spirits meeting a planetary obligation migrate through the same domains on different channels. The shrewd, unfriendly and greedy transmit their negative energy. It's a fierce dominative force but conquerable. The will of the mortal determines that. An ability to decipher bad is a necessary mental power. If not worked on, the body has no idea what forces control it. So, what is good? It's a hard place to reach and challenging to maintain but the reward is eternal. Brahman is one of many names for it. Once found, you are at your center and can see living for what it truly is.

#12:17pm#

Saturday January 12, 2013 9:17pm:_____

Residents of the Third World are becoming more like occupants of District 9- undesired aliens. Meantime those unfortunate people dwell in their mud huts shitting like chimps while talks circulate of their region becoming possession of creditors. Such conglomerates takeover by ripping their newly acquired soil of its resources through paying the dwellers pennies to destroy their homeland. The concept of country has been around since BC times. The leaders were often held in high regard. Now, they are fuck-off half twits, brutal genocidal thugs or good people too often reminded of their fates if they dare improve the status quo. These days, the ballsy get done in by the true rulers. Too many nations are near collapse because of being lured into a game designed for them to lose.

#9:28pm#

Sunday January 13, 2013 11:57pm:————————————————————

Why write? Who reads? The modern writer should strive to make an impact through other means. A multitasking world makes it unwise to stay true to solely text. It leaves one vulnerable to becoming as obsolete as proper spelling and grammar. Once upon a time, in ages we think we're so advanced from, only priests and some lords knew how to articulate. Kings could not script sentences. Words were mainly for verbal context. Is that trend returning? Reading is still a widespread ability but most don't like it. Brains can no longer absorb the rush of content. It's only expected in an information age.

#Monday January 14, 2013 12:12am#

Tuesday January 15, 2013 8:11pm:————————————————————

Stare at pictures of our presidents stacked in order. Follow the path and you will see a few unworthy jerk-offs but mostly gentlemen, scholars and war heroes with John F Kennedy as the mantle piece. After him are sights of corporate owned warmongers. The only unwilling player got smeared by a few rampant Iranians. There it started. That was the beginning of what has led to now. One media sensation brewed American hostilities of wanting to take those "brown bastards" down. It's too easy to mark a radically different culture as the enemy. There is no regard for them while eating Pop Tarts and watching morning newscasts of their suffering. In single file style all those leaders have fueled our fires. Meantime their actions over there piss enough off to achieve welcomed retaliation, which in turn seals justification. Go...look at those faces. Tell me you do not see actors and imposters. Then there's one looking like a grand pharaoh of yesteryear returning to fulfill an ancient manifest destiny.

#8:29pm#

Wednesday January 16, 2013 11:29pm:_____

Finding truth is what they search for, but in doing so their own ver-sions will rise. What is being sought is something they can not morally comprehend. Care gets cremated yearly to produce those results.

#11:35pm#

Sunday January 20, 2013 10:57pm:_____

If I were to die tonight my soul would jump out feeling new and alive. It would no longer be smothered by the hive. Some people would mourn my departure, but, overall not many would give a fuck. The times I'd leave are soon to become ones of begging for mercy. The fate of these lands, which hold my everything, is in the hands of its captors. They will eventually see a need to liquidate. What would I care? It was already Watts out.

#11:06pm#

Monday January 21, 2013 11:58pm:

Where is it said that all is done for the benefit of good? It's a false pretension that too often bites us in the ass, but idiots exist to be taken advantage of. Consensus hopes they never learn otherwise. Rearing them not to defy or question is always a good start. Any brain with some complexity is trainable. It prevents the individual from being complex. In turn the life form is prepped for modern living. That starts with elbows on a table and in due course always leads to getting **FUCKED!** We've all been there. You know when you've exited this phase when you see it in others.

#Tuesday January 22, 2013 12:09am#

Wednesday January 24, 2013 11:48pm:

The past should be seen as nothing but a steamy turd. Looking too much into your times of yore affects the state you're in. Sometimes it creates megalomaniacs but often it whips folk into sad souls walking like broken down dogs. Too many lived moments flutter in brains like shredded plastic bags caught on branches. Those thoughts need to be blown away or restructured. My past no longer harms me. It's not really mine. It wasn't me. Yet, it used to haunt. Overcoming your history allows one to be a significant player in the present. But when is that time and what times will it be in? Because something is being sold does not mean it's made to be bought. Although it does seem as if everything eventually goes.

#Thursday January 25, 2013 12:29am#

Thursday January 31, 2013 11:27pm:_____

Soon the first month of a new year closes and chaos is rising. Doomsday is now 30 seconds closer. Of course the announcement will not be made until a full minute passes, but it can take less than that to jump ahead three. It shows how relative time really is. Everyone has been conditioned to accept the concept of an end and now unhinged is the feeling most in the air. Nothing is working like it used to. We have tired of old ways and too many lack the foresight to set the foundation for new ones. Americans are left living amongst relics that once represented something called culture. Now sterility creeps in. Now we're living in times where fear is the desired reaction to the actions. Now people who want to live, who want to be, who want identity are left being looked upon as undesirable scabs. Freaks we are considered by a society of dumbasses. They have given up everything to serve a system offering less than it ever has and lack comprehension as to why we don't.

#11:44pm#

Monday February 4, 2013 11:53pm:————————————————

Evil is a shapeshifter. Constant transformation keeps it new and trendy. Good remains as the times of Job. It looks as blah as matzo.

#Tuesday February 5, 2013 12:22am#

Tuesday February 5, 2013 11:57pm:————————————————

Something cataclysmic is the best cover up for when shit hits the fan and lies are on the verge of exposure. It's sure as fuck better to lead through tough times than have the arm of the law go tough on you. While fluff and disasters dominate front pages, the extremists have their ears to the ground with what 10 days from now will produce. That's a football like 10 days. It's going to be filled with timeouts and lost yardage. The clock may be dragged down to a point of being shattered.

#Wednesday February 6, 2013 12:04am#

Wednesday February 6, 2013 8:35pm:————————————————

So many people simply want to work and live, but the workers are seen as nothing more than prey. Capitalism has burrowed too deep into humanity. It's now fracking the concept's core. We're left dealing with an infection past points of cure. The objective is to steer clear of the puss.

#8:42pm#

Thursday February 7, 2013 11:07pm:_____

Words alone can read so cold. How they're said can cover up meaning. Someone can talk in rapid fire fashion and never have anything to say. Sometimes a face says plenty on its own and then one hand motion can overrule all. Words, though, hold density by definition. Loose speech serves the same purpose as spandex. Take note of what gets snuck in. You sure don't want it revealed in grotesque fashion.

#Friday February 8, 2013 2:35am#

Saturday February 9, 2013 12:11am:_____

South of Merrick...It's an area that has garnered a lot of attention on Laung Aye-land because of devastation from a recent hurricane. The area no longer goes as south as it used to. FEMA is still present and will probably create reasons to remain. Snow is now mounting on damaged roofs while cold creeps into waterlogged homes. Mold may have ceased its spread but that only gave way to rot. As the observer I am, I write this sitting by my window, which is a one minute walk north of Merrick. I get to see stressed out survivors. I get to hear their stories but all I experienced was wisps of wind from the border of destruction. We're expected to get 2' tonight. When this stuff melts, it will only mark another foiled attempt by nature to free herself from our debauchery. She wants to get back to her organic form. Ahhh... when au naturale, she's one lovely lookin' lady. We all know one thing about the pretty ones- they can be damn hellfire bitches.

Although these thoughts may have come to me they are not solely mine. Well, fuck it! I'm inspired more in not being the only one. It all comes down to how everything is written anyway.

#12:34am#

Monday February 11, 2013 10:39pm:

Novus does non vilis bonus. An old lion has been pressed into submission by rising powers. One was once everyone. Yet, when discussing the people, THEY will eventually have to be the word used. You can't avoid that when dealing with plurality. In fact it's what gives the inspiration to return us to one…. Yeah, back in more advanced times, there was knowledge of truth. It lays in bones and ancient structures. The information, though, still lives. There are ones who know. Who are they?! What does their flesh look like? Why do they hide and keep their secrets? POWER! Oh what a surge it must be to have control over the many! It's never positive, but it marks full success in emulating the gods. They are the ones who initially kept us together. Now our weaknesses get used against us by our own kind. Perhaps those people are in direct contact with the creators. Peter is viewed as the strongest and most loved. He was the one used to build a church on. *Romanorum ero adsuesco assuesco constructum a novus vox ordo*

#11:28pm#

Tuesday February 12, 2013 11:38pm:

Kal Bairo scours lands for the thick ones. He feeds them low energy like a phosphate. It allows for his evil to grow as a lush blanket of suffocating algae. Ah, Kal, many names he has, but he's no man. Brahman is the only fear had by such a dark power.

#Wednesday February 13, 2013 12:55am#

25

Thursday February 14, 2013 11:18pm:

Make a spectacle of the citizens!! That is the new media agenda. Put a few in an awkward spotlight for their absurd acts. **Make them** stand as amusement for the ignorant masses. **Have them** be examples of what no one wants recognition for. **Instill them** with fear of being exposed. **Dose them** with enough paranoia to cease. **Humiliate** the ones caught in the act. Show no love and never report when it is shown.

#11:30pm#

Friday February 15, 2013 5:59pm:

A pair of robins with ruffled plumage were the first seen this year. That was yesterday. The frigid winds made them seem as if they second guessed an early arrival. They were together, though, displaying strength through unity. All current life forms revolve on this abused rock living within the same time frame but experience life on different timelines. When certain frequencies cross, likeminded energies fuse to move forward as a larger whole in more efficient means. A bit of spring revealed itself today. The birds are that much happier.

Blitzed and blown away. What did we do?

#6:16pm#

Saturday February 16, 2013 11:53pm:

Was is only an option of what could have been. One moment possesses an array of possibilities. No single individual controls how seconds connect. Something not happening makes it one of many could'ves we remain unaware of. As long as another possibility is deemed possible, we are always told that the worst will not occur. This is especially true when the stakes are high. If something not taking place means life as usual and sumtin' goin' down means "fuck it we're goners," well, then we will most definitely be told that it will never happen. Pressing pseudo certainty leads to public confidence. It keeps the people at peace. Never mind if it means their remains trapped in volcanic rock.

#11:59pm#

Monday February 18, 2013 11:33pm:

What are we without our vices? Do they deform the person and overpower the soul? Or is what's craved the needed nourishment? One's preference is not always for others but there are few who go without. Do the most spiritual surpass their body's urges? Does their belief in a deity overcome the need for a stiff one? Rock hard vs. god, it's about the animal vs. the supposed human you are. We're told overcoming allows for a strong positive power to flourish, but giving in gives the immediate jolt. At times it reminds us what we like about living and at others it removes us from the like. Either way, forward this globe goes. No matter what you're doing, someone else is experiencing something else until the ultimate is done.

#11:57pm#

Tuesday February 19, 2013 11:59pm:_____

The barking from the Northern portion of the Korean Peninsula has become like that of an obnoxious Chihuahua- constant and unbelievable. At the same time, I've seen no breed bite more people than them little yippers. Problems lay all over. They are ones out of our control, but we can command ourselves. Although never being told so, we are supposed to. If it's done, you will discover answers to questions you were unaware of. Shut off your mind, close your visual aids and connect to your true eye. There you will find what can be done to renovate your self and its immediate surroundings. Ya know, scientists say truths to what they don't fully know because they are paid to be right. You have the ability to discover realities that lay past fact.

#Wednesday February 20, 2013 12:40am#

Thursday February 21, 2013 5:38pm:_____

The brain is the main tool for an individual to establish self but it is not the person. "You" goes far beyond that but the challenge to get there deters the animal within. The earthbound form is an unwilling participant. It's unable to take that ride and will pollute with thought to prevent your temporary departure from form...silence it! Once removed from its barriers, you will gain vision. Seeing with your real eye reveals what's outside and in turn frees one from feeling like an outsider.

#5:58pm#

Friday February 22, 2013 7:15pm:⎯⎯⎯⎯⎯⎯⎯⎯⎯⎯⎯⎯⎯⎯⎯⎯

Uselessness is useful, perhaps more so. It's like debt empowering creditors.

#Saturday February 23, 2013 2:27am#

Monday February 25, 2013 11:23pm:⎯⎯⎯⎯⎯⎯⎯⎯⎯⎯⎯⎯⎯⎯⎯⎯

Slouched backs walking neighborhood sidewalks is too much of an ev-eryday sight. They're broken people oppressed and mangled to points of being owned by Consensus. Their souls are left either tainted or untapped while suffocating in disturbed domains. Zombies they nearly are, but those creatures know how to utilize free will. With US, restric-tions lie within the freedom sold through empty sales pitches from nurtured pricks. My problem is that I stopped buying the product. At the same time, here I am stuck within the confines. I can't escape!! I lack the fame, money or sort after talents to make me appealing for anywhere else. If I had a choice, I'd go to Iceland. Yeah, it's said to be a hip, chill place. It's bound to be cool up there. The skies may be dark, but brightness shines from below. You want freedom? You go there. Remaining here...well, there are bound to be more sights for people reared not to see.

#11:45pm#

Tuesday February 26, 2013 11:58pm:_____

What exactly is faith? Webster's says it is:

1 a : allegiance to duty or a person : loyalty
b (1) : fidelity to one's promises (2) : sincerity of intentions
2a (1) : belief and trust in and loyalty to God (2) : belief in the traditional doc-
trines of a religion
b (1) : firm belief in something for which there is no proof (2) : complete trust

In the end it boils down to being an all or nothing crapshoot. Recognition is a strong motivator. Whether they're flaws, aspirations or inspiration, when people see elements of themselves in others it brings forth allegiance. At the same time, many mothers have faith in their sons no matter what type of delinquent they are. It's odd how others relish in seeing their own fall. Then, of course, faith boils down to where ones religion lies with commitments to old overly edited words. Most of them spell out good virtue but to allow faith to blind surrenders control. Your faith should never stray from yourself. It can guide you to rise. Then people may have faith in you. If so, remember, he who shows courtesy reaps friendship. Followers beware, a lion when hunting does not roar.

#Wednesday February 27, 2013 12:19am#

Wednesday February 27, 2013 11:54pm:_____

There's a glitch in the system of every man. Its exposure occurs when the shield of boyhood is dropped to reveal the fully developed damaged being. No matter what his stature may be, his imperfections are present and they lead to judgment. Does HE overcome them? Does HE let them bring him down? Does HE allow those around him to help compensate or does what plague him become a contagion to burn all who dare to befriend? Too many run rampant not knowing the impact of their actions or have any care; heartless, raw, brutal bulls bred for yesteryear. Times change but the man remains same. Attempts to extinguish lead to laws allowing imprisonment. The hope is to spare the gene pool of continuity. Yet, as a man once said "Nobody's right, if everybody's wrong."

#Thursday February 28, 2013 12:07am#

Thursday February 28, 2013pm 10:06pm:

Sixty five years ago today, I did not exist and I damn well better not be around 65 years from now. A look back shows how love, glory and respect were in the air. Together a great society lived through decades of hardship to reach a point of bright blossom. Those people were the gold said to be lining our streets. In that sense they deserved victory's benefits. Family was their fundamental basis and carrying on tradition was an urge that had to be met. The upshoot of modern conveniences brought forth new found ease. No one realized that their purchases were benefiting the true victors. Back then mass marketing was as much a cherub as a baby roach. Television was its womb and every unit obtained led the way for infestation. Now those still alive from then are mostly burdens to a bankrupt economy. They are locked into promises to take care of them but dare anyone expect to see such treatment again. Sixty five years from now what will there be? Overseers will be surveilling US with their advanced technologies. Employment for these positions is a growing field. Jaded Immigrants, vagrants and dumbfucks are filling them. Those types are perfect for the job because they don't give a damn about anyone and won't tolerate being hassled. They will also always hate how underpaid they are. That doesn't sound too good for US. Respect? Ha! Don't expect that from anywhere. You are a nuisance solely because you exist! Sixty five years from now don't expect to see much of what's currently before you. That includes what's on any community flagpole.

#10:24pm#

Friday March 1, 2013 11:30am:

Round my way there's a strip of road known as Rte 110. If you're looking to purchase a slice of pricy frivality, you'll find it there along with
an obnoxious influx of sales people. They are a terrible breed left living in a squeeze of disrespect. They always need to battle buyers and
tolerate a greedy owner's demands for top dollar. The only sure shot
way to work a floor and maintain subsistence is to substitute emotion
for cash grabs. Deception and mentally arm-baring customers into
submission are the assured survival routes. These repetitive actions
chew on their insides. In winning a battle, more of the self gets lost.
Next time you're in the presence of such a professional stare deep into
those eyes. You will often see a defeated individual broken down to
points of having either the toughest of hides or most permeable skin.
Whichever way, lost souls manipulated by dark powers is all they are.

*The ravens arrived today, the same day as least year. It's an odd thing noticed
only because of notation.*

#11:45am#

Wednesday March 6, 2013 12:27am: *An Ace Perspective*

I close my eyes and feel flight. My ability to overcome has made me
strong. Speaking when silent is hard. It turns me on. The words...those
beautiful genomes may lay flat but are filled with form. Manipulating
language as text leads to raw, naked creations. Whether luscious or
hideous, none are fully mine. They flow inside like electricity and fly
out as an orgasm. After all, this is a daily attempt at procreation. What
creatures the characters add up to is a surprise. Whatever they become, I know I live on here long after the release goes cold.

#1:03am#

Friday March 8, 2013 12:16am:_____

Tears are always shed when the good ones go. People rejoice when the bad guys are done in. If so, why was there recent footage of sad Venezuelans following Hugo Chavez's final moments? Seeing that was as if someone who loved his country and people passed. But he was a monster, right? They cry for him as if he was a hero. After all that Consensus has said, it's an odd sight.

#12:58am#

Sunday March 10, 2013 10:40pm:_____

Too much of modern living is geared toward feeding the inner beast. The more it eats, the larger it grows. Then, like any improper pet, it reaches points of feeling penned up. Contained energy leads to a mental frenzy and internal static. Both leave the mechanism prone to negativity. The more that surges, closer comes victory. Noooo, don't think you're the winner. You move that much closer to losing everything.

The problem with something is that it always needs to be put somewhere. Not everything is fitting to go everywhere if anywhere at all.

#10:50pm#

Monday March 11, 2013 11:52pm:_____

The employee exists to make money for the employer. It's simply how things work. But what is made off of your efforts versus what you go home with is at The Man's discretion and he's not known for generosity. A restaurant owner expects his patrons to pay the help. A doctor flaunts his high end sports car while cutting his staff's hours. A plumber can sit back, schedule appointments and cash the checks his boys bring back. Meantime, they make $10prhr to have days full of fecal fun. I can remember, around 18 months ago or so, citizens rebelling over being treated outright shitty. They were silenced while other nations go as far as ousting or outright killing their leadership. Our powers support that action. Simultaneously they pepper spray, beat and taze their own. "Shut up ya fucks, you have your freedom" is the message their actions send. Yeah, I feel that freedom. Police flex their arm of the law to show how protected they are to do what THEY please. Politicians dictate what their voters can consume and there's a president persuading his citizens to cheer on the surrendering of their rights. What's on the horizon? The clocks have moved forward. Spring is soon to come. 2013 will be hitting full bloom or is that one big BOOM?!

#Tuesday March 12, 2013 12:09am#

Wednesday March 13, 2013 11:54pm:_____

Growth and death are far from two things that go together. In fact that does not apply even in a metaphysical sense. Death in one realm can give way to growth in another but under no circumstances does an entity continue growing while dying. No, then we see crumbling. Then one gives way to another, but what? Death is not what this day brought, is it? Illustrious blooms often precede decay. Remembrance begins once that final second ceases. History proves we develop horrible cases of amnesia. The future is always tomorrow and no day is ever the same. What traits and abilities one has may be the last others will see. It's memory that keeps us alive. It's memory that keeps us alive. It's memory that keeps us alive.

#Thursday March 14, 2013 12:06am#

Thursday March 14, 2013 1:46pm:_____

Virtue is not religion! It is what we're supposed to develop. The teachings of wrong and right can be paraphrased in many ways. The effectiveness of their implementation is integral to reaching adulthood. Age defines such status as being under the premonition that because you are human makes you superior. Actions matter more. Kinds of people showing kindness solely to their kind only means their kind is mean. Reaching out to the ruthless shows you are foolish. Believing all you are told makes you a defeated fool. You are energy, which means that's what you project. Like hydrogen, particles want to unite. Look around you, who you're surrounded by is what you are.

#1:58pm#

Our hearts beat longing to open.
Our hearts beat longing to open.
They follow the goodness we feel within.
We forget that demons rule these times.
Misery is their oxygen.
To maintain healthy production,
their most powerful attack is
the corruption of love.
Yet our hearts beat longing to open

Friday March 15, 2013 11:54pm:_____

The complexity of our kind is brought on by what's forced upon us. These impositions lead to releasing anxieties on one another. A look back shows times when people could meet and love one another for a lifetime. That's frowned upon now. With marriage comes divorce. With both comes an emotional rollercoaster designed to stress systems. More satisfaction is had with inflicting hurt. True love was too innocent. A malevolent need was seen to penetrate it. Once uncoiled, its integrity diminished. Now, feelings get used for manipulation. Love is the real heroin. Its glory leads to a cruel addiction. The source gets highs from cutting off supply. Self empowerment is the fastest gain in dealing this junk. Imagine a girl being surprised on her birthday with cake and candles and her dumping the dude in between chewing it down.

#Saturday March 16, 2013 12:21am#

Yet my heart beats longing to open

35

Saturday March 16, 2013 10:45pm: ———————————————

Negativity is a low frequency high octane force that operates best on a 50/50 ratio of mental and physical. In other words, after it degrades the psyche and breaks down the body. Positivity operates at much higher levels. They are hard ones to reach but everything is more so free flow the closer one gets to a pinnacle. Someone taller could be right next to you but living in a world far below.

#10:56pm#

Sunday March 17, 2013 11:42pm: ———————————————

Sticking to the issued script solely means you are a character in someone else's game. Identity has been replaced with sterility and to who's gain? How happy are you? Where does your happiness hail from? Discovering that reveals your persona. Someone else finding it becomes enabled. Unlock the source of what makes someone smile and you earn their commitment. Please the people and they become glad to be around you. Stifle, oppress and/or compress and you leave them depressed. What's the gain? Why is it the oft chosen way?

#Monday March 18, 2013 12:00am#

Monday March 18, 2013 11:56pm:———————————————

Gravity keeps us down but what we gravitate around leads to who we are surrounded by. Does kissing a foe allow for good graces or a tighter grip? What leads to one having dislike toward another and then how are there some loved by all? It's hard to have hatred for anyone that does not possess any. It's rare to find someone who brings out the good in everyone. Saint, I guess, is the word applied to such individuals but I need no church for confirmation. I know the preeminent who once walked with me. Their spirits surround in wait for mine. I know the good ones alive around me now, their souls shine. However, I know not what I fully am!

#Tuesday March 19, 2013 12:10am#

Tuesday March 19, 2013 11:37pm:———————————————

What are the answers? Questions could be asked with confidence if solutions were known. Give me all of them! I would never directly reveal any. A writer needs to be an inspirer. Readers must be made to think or else the job is not being done. A waiter got angry with me because I only ordered miso soup to go. The total came to $2.07. I gave him $5.10. He gave me my change on a tip tray. I took back $3.01.

#11:55pm#

Monday March 25, 2013 11:31pm:_____

The streets rumble in their everyday way shaking and suffocating the earth as our responsible monstrosities emit their poisons. They're sooo antiquated, yet still the dominant option. Creation starts with a thought and not every one thunk should come to be. A solution to one problem usually gives way to new complications. With automobiles, unfortunately pollution was never considered and road kill... well, that's an overlooked after effect of progress. Them silly critters, they have yet to adapt to the idea of a moving object not responding to the works of nature. An opossum playing its game will only become a pizza!

So ends simple cognition.

Now let's flow toward abysmal contemplation.

Someone came up with the idea of annihilating regions and the wildfires of evil, rage and hate made that come to be. It was perfectly capped off with Oppenheimer quoting Vishnu. Since then, we've seen change. Citizens are now nothing but subjects subjected to the actions of nations that no longer possess nationalism! Like silly kittens, most of us are left innocent and unaware. This only means that there will be plenty of slices to go around.

#Tuesday March 26, 2013 12:00am#

Wednesday March 27, 2013 1:34am:_____

There is a desire for the burning sort of action. It's growing stronger. The rage is smoldering and being fed daily doses of hot air. Of course, all we feel is the cold of another turbulent March, but heat... that's rising everywhere else. Anarchy of the highest degree can break at any moment. All we need is one slight mishap. Do ya wanna see the day when all flames fly?! I dread seeing such pointless death but I know there are ones who drool for it or merely view it as meeting goals. They solely care about their closed hearts beating after heartlessness prevails. Blood is such a pretty shade of red and spreads better than water colors. With it running through them, rivers will look how the ones on Mars probably did. Its splatter effect on roadways would be so art deco that one may think Andy Warhol returned for one last masterpiece. Grizzled skin will be a pretty touch and maimed cadavers always add a nice medieval flare. Yeah, think of it all as a renaissance festival. It would be a pretty cheap one to create as there is an abundance of needed materials. Turning them into the desired effect will be as insignificant as downing a hamburger. Hahaha...don't worry about seeing this come to be. Chances are high you'll already be part of the decor. Our kind will live on though. They will be ones who have shed humanity. Hail those great beings! For they worship god and make us believe their way is good.

#1:50am#

Thursday March 28, 2013 11:54pm (for Leon):＿＿＿＿＿＿＿＿＿

Truth runs disguised as darkness in the shadows of the moon. Reality is revealed to those who can see beyond what eyes enable. The spirits play in comfort on an Earth that was theirs long before we came to be. The form they wish to take is at their discretion. So is their desire to disband. Humans are utilized to tell the story of all. It assures that very few minutes get lost to present a nearly absolute pallet of existence. Each minor fragment leads to giving details of a larger tale. In that sense, we are all the writers. But then, who is the reader?

#Friday March 29, 2013 12:13am#

Saturday March 30, 2013 11:57pm:＿＿＿＿＿＿＿＿＿

Shhhhh...listen and you can hear the whispers rise. Mumbles they will become. Foreseen realities will manifest. It's scary to know that it has begun, but it's been moving like the roll of a glacier. Now, it seems ready for landslide. The hills will shake soon enough. It's a fire running through that leads to these words. His kind carried on the beliefs and waited for their turn to count. Possession has now taken root. So soon the decision does not seem right. More wrong is on the way because guess what...the good fight has ceased being fought.

Words are math. When stacked right, they lead to conclusions. Permanent they are, unless edited.

#Sunday March 31, 2013 12:21am#

Sunday March 31, 2013 11:30pm:————————————————————

The rain in Juarez this time of year must be the soothing misty type filled with renewal as it leads to blossoming spring flowers; peaceful, beautiful, jovial. Chilling drops are all that fall on Northeastern terrains as a reminder to everyone that March has yet to quit its turbulence. Varying storms can still arise long after a calendar flip. Anything is possible in these times but don't bank on positives. Perennials do reach points where they stop rising. Then weeds take over. They represent undesired life, yet grow unaware of that perception. When yanked from the ground they're left clueless to why they were killed. Juarez is not free of such things but the people feel as such while looking toward happiness. That is until the pollutants and parasites lodged in their bodies do away with them.

#11:41pm#

Wednesday April 3, 2013 11:55pm:————————————————————

In order for a connection to be made one simply needs to find the right adapter. It's elementary for any craftsman, but advanced skill is no longer enforced. Too many people throw themselves out there with hopes of gaining only attraction. Then they have no idea what they are bringing in. What's discovered past the chemicals is seldom the initial presumption. Your special one could be an experienced journeyman using implements to appear as an angel, but really the demon to your existence. These usurpers unleash their darkness with every thrust you allot. Who you attract, defines yourself. You may not be a dark soul, but you may be a fiend. Then you're seen as weak enough to devour. How do you know? Well, if you even have to question, then you are already a candidate. However, your certainty must not derive from ignorance. It must also be a key you do not share.

The geese have begun their return. It would be raining feathers if they were 32.8 ° N 35.6 ° E.

#Thursday April 4, 2013 ???#

Thursday April 4, 2013 11:59pm:————————————————————

Almost means it didn't happen. Like, the Nazis almost had the A-bomb. The Cuban Missile Crisis almost got way ugly. Al Gore was almost president. Millions of people were almost spared having their lives affected in disastrous ways. Millions more were almost able to continue living. No, instead atrocities occurred. Of course the ones most responsible will never answer for their actions. They did everything in the name of humanity only to wipe their asses on the humans they used as examples to protect. Yet the façade carries on. It's weathered with missing pickets but still intact enough to lure believers. Those same folk will eventually become ones who turn in others.

#Friday April 5, 2013 12:43am#

Saturday April 6, 2013 10:01pm:——————————————————

Wounds set in suddenly. They leave the insides abused and, often, exposed. The pain remains registered and leads to one seeking refuge. But is there a need to stay in it? Living requires knowing how to dance in the rain. If you don't try, you will eventually be forced.

#10:15pm#

Monday April 8, 2013 12:11am:——————————————————

Confusion lies in yesterday's thought, but that can be said of any day. In these need-to-know times too much goes anonymous. There's a masquerade involved with every move.

#12:33am#

Monday April 8, 2013 11:45pm:——————————————————

Anyone is free to believe what they please but everyone should be aware of how far imagination goes. Fuck it all! Believe in nothing. Live solely by your senses.

#11:54pm#

Tuesday April 9, 2013 11:23pm:_____

Black smoke comes from a high rise at a perfect moment to symbol-
ize something to someone. What? It's more about how coincidences
happen in ways where they do not seem coincidental. Black smoke
rising when darkness is spoken...why? It's an example of how in-
terwoven the hive really is. Black smoke from a rooftop on the first
beautiful spring day. It comes from many places but this puff
leads to wonder. There was a need to disclose what was said. A response came from other dimensions through sources that only speak
truth. Black smoke, black smoke, it's impossible to forget. Where we
are is only where others can roam.

#11:37pm#

Thursday April 11, 2013 1:31am:_____

The moment it feels as if there's a return to "normalcy" is when one
is caught off guard. There is no "normal!" It's a figment fluttering
in the brains of those who wish not to feel what surrounds. Basic
standards are set for ones to reach and abide by but clinging to them
leads to overlooking your own calling. Nothingness lies in "normalcy." It's an area to start paving your way to where fate intends. No
guarantees come with creating such a road. It's about you challenging your own powers to give your visions reality. To do so, you must
never lose sight of where you are, where you're supposed to be and
who you need to become.

#2:04am#

Friday April 12, 2013 11:59pm:

The endgame is obvious. The money men drool for collapses. Do they only think of swiping the whole pie? History reveals how divided portions can become. The days of hammer and sickle still loom. Right now, the most noted wall makers could be getting ready to build a new one seen from the moon and beyond. Current actions, along with the ones to follow, are bound to bring forth bad karma. Greed reaching its epitome simply has to have consequences.

#Saturday April 13, 2013 12:20am#

Saturday April 13, 2013 10:28pm:

The headlines fly by saying different things but too many mount to meaning: RED ALERT. Minds seem to absorb such info but choose to store it like fat molecules produced by glutenized empty carbs. Keep consuming the shit but look the other way to its after effects. Enjoy the personal thrills minutes bring but remain naive to how they're piling toward disaster. The problem lies with hopelessness being too dominant. It's amazing how billions can feel as if the matter is out of their hands. In many ways the big picture is, but it can be altered. No, it's not about grouping together to make a stand. Masses make scenes. Individuals can infiltrate. If everyone took time to work on themselves, it would create a stronger social tapestry. Don't eat defeat! It only keeps Consensus content.

#10:45pm#

Sunday April 14, 2013 11:51pm:

When the spotlight shines your imperfections get exposed. Scrutiny prevails over such a moment. Your response makes you vulnerable to failure- a five lane roadway filled with gridlock. You can always prevent taking such a route. Everyone notices someone who stands strong.

#Monday April 15, 2013 12:00am#

Monday April 15, 2013 8:22pm:————————————————

False flags fly higher than those we pledge our allegiance to. Terror is a powerful concoction. Panic and paranoia are the main ingredients to produce enough fright for unassuming hosts. Sporadic dosings of horror prevent the decline of daily apprehension and enhance coercion to shave away rights for a smooth layer of protection. Trust citizens may have had in one another gets foregone and placed more in possession of our overseers. They're craving to gain full authority. It's the ultimate ego stroke packed with plenty of double-time opportunities.

#8:30pm#

Wednesday April 18, 2013 11:55pm:————————————————

The present is not the past and the future remains in ways unforeseen. Yet so much is apparent. That chaos sprinkles down more than acid rain. It painlessly erodes the morale fiber of our societal structure; then our nerves. Then it flares. Then it pains. Then it kills. It's not a fast demise. The infected are intentionally allowed to menace. Your actions may not be ones to serve you as much as dark powers you're entirely unaware of. If so, your well being is something they care little for. It's about what you can do for them before you're done away with.

#Thursday April 19, 2013 12:14am#

Friday April 19, 2013 10:24pm:_____

Confusion develops when walking in circles. There's a need to wonder why the same keeps being seen. Wander Lane is a road long since walked. It exists for one to eventually choose a route. Staying committed to the course may not lead to anticipated results. All choices have consequences. It's the amount of extremes that should hold relevance. Surrendering so much to achieve so little and all of it only negative is the foolishness of youth. Sharp minds with clumsy feet and cold hearts can stir the underworld to points of it surfacing for the gain of no one but to some thing.

#10:36pm#

Saturday April 20, 2013 4:20pm:_____

Outside, the people on the inside stare at outsiders walking past. Polarity is evident between such types. The strangest metamorphosis is seen from one giving into Consensus. Suddenly there is the disposal of a faction that an association to was once displayed with pride. Those times become a time to grow away from for proof of being a grownup. Meantime, misery sets in. Lost and owned those people become. Yet, for some odd reason, they see themselves as buyers but not of what they long for.

#4:24pm#

Sunday April 21, 2013 10:54pm:⎯⎯⎯⎯⎯⎯⎯⎯⎯⎯⎯⎯

The wars over who is supplying the right and real information are more a battle for attention than accuracy. To become ones source for something means empowerment. With that comes the ability to influence thought, which always leads to some sort of control. All the news moguls of the past knew this. Don't think that knowledge died with 'em. Yet, as with all originals, progression gets substituted with emulation. Success gets stale when too many play it the same way. The formulas become so apparent that amateurs get seen as pros. Then only the dumb still believe. Those who think for themselves realize there's no need for TV.

#11:08pm#

Monday April 22, 2013 11:59pm:⎯⎯⎯⎯⎯⎯⎯⎯⎯⎯⎯⎯

Guesswork usually leads to a right or wrong scenario. The consequences of your decision should be weighed. The actions always need to be thought out. Commitment to the move needs to be 100%. Then there's a need to accept potential failure and live past it. The wrong moves are ones you'll never forget but future actions can eliminate them from public thought. Too often a dome of artificial reality surrounds. You can always back out of it but don't guess so. There's a need to remain committed.

#Tuesady April 23, 2013 12:20am#

Tuesday April 23, 2013 11:55pm:————————————————

Revealing secrets of self leads to growth of mind and soul. The body grows with the more it keeps in. Ultra wide it gets as stress builds and a need to eat overwhelms. It's a futile attempt of distraction. Releasing relieves. The problem is the ears of who obtain the info. Anything said in another's presence is prone to scrutiny. It makes known elements of the true being and gives way to vulnerability. What stops the holder of your words from disclosing them and destroying you? Either use wisdom to choose who you discuss your inner feelings with or pay for the service.

#Wednesday April 24, 2013 12:12am#

Wednesday April 24, 2013 11:58pm:————————————————

Is there time to rest in times of unrest? Disturbances are growing into potentially prophetic moments. Ronald Reagan would occasionally mention zany concepts of more advanced creatures intervening on our daily insanity to annihilate us. What would we do? How fast would we unite as one race and forget the bullshit? Terrorist attacks, nuclear plant explosions, US dropping those two bombs...damn, Japan alone must radiate an intergalactic glow showcasing Earthling crudeness. We've fucked shit up! Yet because the sun has always risen we presume it will tomorrow. Believing we're alone in an otherwise dead universe is the modern version of thinking the world is flat. So, let's spin back to Ronnie's silliness. We would become one without hesitation thinking in our usual innocent way that everyone is doing it for the better of good. Perceived perception is the best tool for deception. Rest assured there will be no leaders battling them aliens amongst their fellow citizens.

#Thursday April 25, 2013 12:38am#

Thursday April 25, 2013 11:44pm:_____

The way to finding a getaway feels within grasp. What is it that you're reaching for? Temptation is a perverse impulse. It leaves its mark somewhere on you while crossing the wires of your psyche.

#Friday April 26, 2013 12:16am#

Sunday April 28, 2013 9:50pm:_____

A flip back of recent weeks reveals the continuity of disturbances. Nuances of horror keep piling. They help maintain social insecurity.

#10:03pm#

Tuesday April 30, 2013 11:54pm:_____

As secure we are told to be, insecurity prevails. Its presence does not arise from apparent threats as much as how we're being protected. Are they on our side? We feel more like victims to be taxed, taken advantage of and deemed guilty for any made up infraction. We need to trust at a time when vulnerable but we're given no reason to.
We need to come together and show love but our imposed stresses keep us divided. We need to freely express ourselves but the laws bind us down. We need our military and leaders to be there for what is supposedly US...
BUT THEY'E NOT REALLY OURS!.

#Wednesday May 1, 2013 12:04am#

Wednesday May 1, 2013 11:45pm:————————————————

Everyone wants everything there way. It's baffling how we don't
see conflicts arise in the actual everywhere. Then again, peace feels
present only because we've become accustomed to living in tension.
Every moment brings on more problems. Few get exposed until they
mount to big ones. A shock effect makes for better ratings.

#Thursday May 2, 2013 12:03am#

Monday May 6, 2013 11:43pm:————————————————

Abuses too often get us through a day. Substances and animal-like
activity are needed to mask apprehension. We're shown how to be by
others and wind up following the same thorny paths set by Consensus. A stranger may have shown you the way. It's actions we follow.
After all, a monkey still thrives somewhere under our hides.

#Tuesday May 7, 2013 12:12am#

Tuesday May 7, 2013 8:26pm:————————————————

Pastel-like chemtrails line a sunset sky as if they're pretty, happy
whisks that once came from the blades of Bob Ross. Offsets of yellows
from dandelions taking over lawns and baby geese shitting on them
crisscross around polluted lakes. All of life is giving off a harmoni-
ous hallelujah! I stare at this tapestry with the sense that it could
be THE last. It would be so ironic to see destruction come under a
lovely spring sky doming the emergence of so much newness. Sound
and vision are not two components in sync with one another. They
are independent functions. Each has potential to deceive. Often it's
one and not the other. So there is always the possibility of full comprehension. Bewilderment, though, too often overpowers. Pixels and
decibles overload cortexes to persuade us to think their way. Listen
then look. At other times look then listen. Only after both are com-
pleted should it lead to thought.

#8:52pm#

Wednesday May 8, 2013 11:56pm:_____

May is doing its usual flyby. It makes me wonder what the months are like on Mars. That dinged up red rock has become a craze. The life forms already discovered are intriguing. They are the mutated survivors of more bountiful times. These morphons have either hard exoskeletons or thick scaly skin to protect them in environments with little atmosphere. It's amazing!! Oh wait... no, there is nothing up there or ever was. It may appear that way, but, ya know, it's kinda like how people who recently departed the Stone Age transformed those rocks into spellbinding structures that modern technology still can not replicate. Right, they were simply primitive folk that had nothing better to do than build in the day and look at stars every night. They must have all been asinine autistics. Damn, the blah blah Consensus bullshit carries on for decades and never evolves. We're always expected to believe and go about a futile existence. Why think? Others can do that for us and we're told they know better. Tidbits too tiny to reveal truth are best for the children. If they knew any more they would never again listen.

#Thursday May 9, 2013 12:15am#

Monday May 13, 2013 5:15pm:_____

Areas within get damaged and leave fragile parts vulnerable to agitation. There lies the awful everything. It's not a disease but it can definitely become a cancer. It's hard to detect because of the "it" never being "the" same. Self diagnosis is always needed. Treatments must be pursued. That is a seldom mentioned duty. Too often people expect their states of operation to be regulated by others. That leaves them like a balloon floating with no control and vulnerable to burst from the slightest of changes. Be your own mechanic. Get to know how all the components operate. Realize when you need assistance from ones who may know better, but always attempt to help yourself.

#6:20pm#

Wednesday May 15, 2013 11:02pm:_____

How long can one remain content hiding behind someone else's tune? Too often music masks the self. Songs serve as surrogates to get us through by enthralling senses the same way every time. In turn they prevent the flow of real feeling. I should be listening to my own tune, as you should too. No, I'm not saying you listen to me. I am saying we should all listen to ourselves. In saying that, though, I am influencing your train of thought. At least that's what I'm thinking right now. So does that mean in talking to my self I expect you to acknowledge me? No, it's not about me vexing for your attention as much as everyone. There are tools reserved for specialist in their fields. They are only issued after one proves how the job can be done without them.

#11:26pm#

Sunday May 19, 2013 10:24pm:_____

The center of attention should seldom be your focal point. There lies the ultimate diversion.

#10:25pm#

Tuesday May 21, 2013 11:09pm:_____

Possessing an overload of emotion in the 21st Century is the Achilles Heal of our kind. Seldom is elation not pyrite. It's someone toying with your innocence to get something out of you. There is no care anymore. That was left somewhere in the 1900's. It will linger until us final remnants subside. Yet, now, it's more so vestigial. Ahhhh-hhh....I wanna let go of apathy, but it's needed to maintain control and prevent damage. Vapor trails must be emitted to keep away potential problems. In turn, I remain locked in solitary. Pain too often overrides pleasure. It grinds souls until they scream for release.

#11:28pm#

Why does my heart beat longing to open?

53

Wednesday May 22, 2013 11:28pm:_____

Humidity is sticking to the skin complete with gnats swarming in a ball of annoyance. Summer has yet to arrive but they're ready to play. Some may be chillin' with their parents who survived a mild winter and were part of a huge baby boom thanks to the hurricane. Soon we're set to get zapped with the tail end of storms that rocked the Midwest. Maybe one day a sinkhole will appear somewhere on St. Mark's. It would signify how done in the area already is. Not many would care anyway. The natural disaster has become so commonplace that people are beginning to become immune. Towns destroyed, residents dead, millions of dollars issued for relief aid, (yawn...) might as well add a few hundred corpses in the Middle East to that humdrum news.

#Thursday May 23, 2013 12:00am#

Saturday May 25, 2013 10:17pm:_____

So the ghosts surround. Their essence holds together like that of mighty Jupiter. There are atmospheres within both hemispheres. They border each other in a semi-permeable sense. There is no crossing over as much as busting through. So many souls crumble while smacking against an endless wall. While in their pupa phase they never met potential. It only starts here. We're each born with the capability of reaching eternity. Responsibility and sincerity are required. If applied, you'll find that your next destination is in a near distant land and it's a long short way to get there.

#10:44pm#

Tuesday May 28, 2013 8:05pm:——————————————

Body odor fills the Penn Station waiting room. The homeless are getting more creative with making the place home. They've caught on that all it takes to use the area is having a ticket and one of those is good for 60 days. Hell, a half hour's of street work invested into two months rent is a damn good deal! There's even a bathroom included. At certain times urinals are free enough to use as showers. Way back in times I never saw, cigarette smoke would have helped mask this stench. Now Smokers are left persecuted and financially raped for giving into corporate seduction. The addict is the creation of the powers-that-be. They know how far they can go. Why not put a ban on B.O.? How's about making it illegal to be homeless? Now that's a solution!! Get all those stinky bastids back in their homes. Either that or collect and tag them like stray dogs with a daily countdown to their time. Cruelty I bring today because of what I feel in the air- persecution of the people for being people.

#8:27pm#

Thursday May 30, 2013 11:57pm:——————————————

Pop, pop, pop... new species emerge every year, yet we're told they've been here as long or longer than ones we've known of forever. There are now mega-sized pink slugs. These goonie-goo things have gone unknown for centuries but we're told they've always been in the Australian mountain ranges. Wow, a new foot long invertebrate looking sooo alien. The question is how much so? Science believes the seeds of life were brought from space. If so, well, first off, there is proof that life exists somewhere else, but also, what are we bringing back? Well, fuck it! We've already proven how little care is had for this planet.

#Friday May 31, 2013 12:13am#

Friday May 31, 2013 11:59pm:⎯⎯⎯⎯⎯⎯⎯⎯⎯⎯⎯⎯⎯⎯⎯⎯⎯

So ends another May. These 31 days get chugged like a tall boy. The curtain is now open for a performance that could possibly top any before. Everyone can go outside to see it if they dare leave their confines and become vulnerable to the new laws. Guilt is all the cops go out looking for and it's been made easier to find. Fuck, why is this becoming real? We are the ones who pay for the protection and they have a field day shitting on US. And that's not me and my kind as much as everyone, everywhere. A flag flies only to remind us of the past.

#Saturday June 1, 2013 12:14am#

Monday June 3, 2013 11:27pm:⎯⎯⎯⎯⎯⎯⎯⎯⎯⎯⎯⎯⎯⎯⎯

Pushed we all are to points of feeling like a school of fish prodded by predators into a bait ball. It could be paranoia taking its toll. Nothing is wrong. ALL is well. We're good and none of what I say is true.

#11:43pm#

Thursday June 6, 2013 11:57pm:⎯⎯⎯⎯⎯⎯⎯⎯⎯⎯⎯⎯⎯⎯⎯

Where you came from does not hold as much relevance as to who you've become. What is the point in holding on to memories you have no pride in? People are the biggest contributors to having effects on the lives of others and that often leads to disdain. Love is all we ever want, but it's seldom there. Looking too hard for something often makes it impossible to find. We get caught up in our own bullshit. We make ourselves stumble. Everyone has the ability to walk tall, even if they lack mobility. You simply need to tell yourself to. Your calling is attempting to get your attention at all times. Simply answer it and begin the climb. You always know when you're doing things right because that's when love finds ya. Never expect it at any other time. Then you'll only wind up with someone deterring you from where ya need to be. Move forward. Take the initiative. Something always comes of it.

#Friday June 7, 2013 12:22am#

Sunday June 9, 2013 11:28pm:⎯⎯⎯⎯⎯⎯⎯⎯⎯⎯⎯⎯⎯⎯⎯

Arm the rebels fighting against their rulers for the supposed betterment of ones we care little about. Never mind how weak their nations will be after the smoke clears. They'll be looking for handouts. We know who will gladly give.

#11:34pm#

Monday June 10, 2013 10:47pm:

Immediate gratification is always in need. Waiting imposes messages of inferiority. Everyone must be served in a way where they feel important. Satisfaction is essential in one's life. Special we all are; as unique as a snowflake that crashes to the ground and settles to eventually become dirty slush.

So much can be written about the beautiful mystery of footprints in the sand but one damn piece turned the whole concept into a tacky wall mount.

#11:36pm#

Wednesday June 12, 2013 11:39pm:

God is love. God is love. God is love- Close your eyes. Repeat. Don't think. Let the words loop. Leave the mind void. *God is love. God is love. God is love-* Let the words loop. Make the mental chatter fade. Let the words loop. This body is yours and **YOU** have full control. *God is love. God is love. God is love-* Let the words loop, let the words loop, let the words loop. The blue light, you should be seeing it. Follow it deep. Suddenly you'll be able to see sights of higher plains settled in mountains where only you can climb to, not the components that encase. *God is love. God is love. God is love-* Let the words loop. Let go. Let them release you. Because if god is love, then love is god and only there can you truly feel it.

#Thursday June 13, 2013 12:34am#

Thursday June 13, 2013 11:59pm:_____

What was Hitler? He has become an emblem of iniquity but we'll never know what creature hid behind those blue eyes. What was it like living while news of his wrath was still wet ink? I once asked my grandmother that. Dementia had already set in, but as Swissed as her brain was those mental receptors jumped back fast. "You knew to be afraid" she said. A blatantly wicked man taking over Europe was enough to make knees shake overseas, but we watched France fall. In modern times was there fear of Sadaam Hussein? No, we laughed at him and now his execution is a quick piss break clip on YouTube. Do we even know anything about this guy Bashar al-Assad? Do we care? No! There's no fear, humor or regard. How common is awareness of where his Syrian lands lie? Well, if you're uncertain, let's put it like this: it's in the way of the most direct route for a pipeline from Baghdad to Europe. That's one of many fringe benefits we have no care for, but the ones who control US sure do. As for us, well if we are to ever have our grandkids ask what it was like living through all the wars, our Swissed up brains might reply back saying "Snooki."

Yeah, I went there! In decades to come who else will be seen as the figurehead of these plastic times?

#Friday June 14, 2013 1:12am#

Tuesday June 18, 2013 10:29pm:_____

What is it? I feel it creeping like a centipede heading up my crotch. Is it a demon? If so, it's a crafty one attempting to become a virus to my soul. Threat detected. Now it must be fought. I DO NOT SERVE SUCH POWERS!

#10:37pm#

Wednesday June 19, 2013 6:22pm:

Geminis continue dancing in their glory despite this being yet another jacket weather evening. Cold is prevailing longer than I ever recall. Demons lurk. They've been crossing my path on a daily basis. I sense them. They know this. Therefore they stalk to weigh me down. The easy prey has long since been digested. One must be weary. Much more is at play than we have ever experienced. Perhaps that goes for the history of our kind. Never before have the people been muted by the media. Never before can eyes creep in everywhere. Never before has destruction had so much ease. Messages are being sent from the other side at an impulsive pace. It makes deciphering them a challenge. This must be urgent. I fear we will all know what I mean too soon.

#6:56pm#

Thursday June 20, 2013 6:53pm:

The sun is still beaming high. Our mighty giver of life is overlooking all she feeds. She's prepping to reveal her full splendor. When she does, it's kind of like the pope coming, except her holiness is unavoidable to feel. Her glory, her warmth, her love wraps around us. Fuck, quit the poetic personification! What's up there is responsible for all of down here! Is that a challenge for one to realize? We are staring god in the face every day! There is the power source of the universe and it's angry. Perhaps it's feeling neglected. Perhaps it doesn't like how we're tending to our elderly Earth mother. Perhaps we're simply pets that it's tired of tending to.

#7:16pm#

photo credit: Nate Watts

Friday June 21, 2013 5:17am:

Here, I'm set in meditation, naked and alone. My feet were the first to leave their marks on fresh shoreline. Desolation thrives in full splendor as I prepare in wait for the arrival of mother energy's golden radiance. Calmness falls. Answers will come. Is an alienated freak really the only one who cares to experience such religion?

5:41am

Boom...there she stands before me with the power of billions of A-bombs. I stare directly into her gaze mesmerized, meditating, moving while in stagnation. Greatness still exists and the gods are real but only love is god.

8:16pm

Vapor trails have ceased emission! That can lead to danger, but I was recently told that love finds you when you're on the right road. Two spirits reunite to revive an ancient dance in new form. One is younger but an elder. The other with back pages no longer relevant. The demon revealed herself through an ambush attempt and left pissed. The sun sets to bring forth an evening with possible peril. However, this dim sets in with me knowing I have been released from solitary.

#8:30pm#

Postscript- *EVERYDAY WRITING: A Deconstruction of the Human Hive*

So concludes our first journey. Uncertainy lies if we will ever have another or when. With that in mind, here's two more...

photo credit: Joe Bear

Monday July 22, 2013 9:05pm:————————————————————

"Oooh yeah!" There were few wrestlers more known and hailed than the Macho Man Randy Savage. Teaming up with the Hulkster is what made him the colorful sensation loved by millions. There was a time, though, where he was a hated bad ass misogynist shithead. Fuck, he'd beat down his opponents in a way where it actually seemed real! The exceptional fire he put behind his character earned him getting scripted into a role garnering fanfare. Then his past went overlooked. No matter what one once was, becoming a hero often earns admiration and, at minimum, makes it hard to stay angry at someone. This gimmick has worked in wrestling for decades. Those steroidal nearly nude men go out there being more so illusionists than athletes. Deep down the audience knows this, but still chooses to believe . Good deeds always earn their forgiveness. That's nearly the basis for humanity. It's a simple concept to comprehend and an even easier one to dishonor. Everyone knows Shakespeare once said "All the world's a stage." It only took close to 500 years for his words to be soooo damn blatant.

#9:31pm#

Thursday July 25, 2013 9:16pm:———————————————

How long is one's past supposed to plague when only the present mat-
ters? Is it fair for someone to remain a prisoner from moments lost in
time? They are considered truth but change has its effects. Do we expect
a butterfly to return to being a caterpillar? No, but the argument can also
be that the caterpillar's transformation is expected. Anything outside
of the norm always stands a chance of rejection but renewal deserves its
acknowledgements. Change can reach points where a new being emerges.
Must the person be whipped with reminders of the past self? The new
one integrates with a distinct beat. Some people feel it and catch on.

#9:43pm#

... A psychic once said there will be three.

#30#

Nathaniel Watts

photo credit: Scott Greer

Made in the USA
Charleston, SC
17 January 2015